This journal belongs to:

· ·

Gradma Your Story is a Gift Journal

**A book for grandmother to fill out, remember her life
& share favorite memories with grandkids**

2nd Edition - April 2021

 @adaytoremember_journals
✉ adaytoremember.journals@gmail.com

INDEX

Introduction

Writing about our memories and life stories is a way to keep them forever. Loving, remarkable, funny memories and stories of overcoming challenges can be real treasures, serve as inspiration and even become lessons to our loved ones when they need it.

How many things happen in our lives that we would like to leave on record so that children and grandchildren could get to know and learn a little more about us and from what we have already lived?

Remember the first time you carried your grandchildren?
And the first time you baked a cake together?
And when he / she fell and you helped them to feel better?
And remember when you were a child and your mother taught you so many things that you would also like to teach your grandchildren?

Our life is full of moments that deserve to be shared and this journal was designed to help you do just that.

Sharing your memories and stories with your grandchildren can be wonderful for you and for them, do you know why?

- Your grandchild will realize that your story and the story of your ancestors relates to their own;
- Writing helps organize the "shelves" of our mind and puts events in perspective, on a timeline;
- Writing also make you re-live happy moments, feel the joy once again; and it sometimes helps "heal" from past events, too;
- Your grandchildren's understanding of the past helps them to accept themselves as they are, learn that their roots impacts the way they are,
- Capturing your memories on paper will bring you joyful & funny memories that will now make others laugh!

With this journal, you will give your grandchildren an opportunity to learn about their family's history, an inspiration to live happy moments the way you did, and examples of strength that will help them overcome life's obstacles and challenges.

Let's write some beautiful memories and inspiring stories together?

Before you get started we'd like to introduce ourselves and THANK YOU *for buying this journal!*

We are 2 high school friends just starting a journey of entrepreneurship.
(We're now "grown ups", moms; Carla is based in the USA, and Milena in Brazil).

We are challenging ourselves to create 52 journals this year, ~1 per week!
We are so grateful for your support so far, and we invite you to follow our journey.

Our promise: *to make* EVERY *customer happy*

We hope and believe that this journal will help you remember, organize
and share your memories & stories with the next generations of your family.
A gesture of love and affection that can inspire the lives of the people you love.

But if for any reason you are not satisfied with your journal, please contact us directly;
we will do our best to make you happy!

Your REVIEW *means a lot to us!*

And especially if you like this journal, would you please give us a couple minutes of your time
and write a review on Amazon?

As we write this, this journal is brand new and has no ratings or reviews on Amazon,
so each new one makes a BIG difference.

Your honest review is a big encouragement for us, new creators and sellers, to keep going.
And it helps other people find our product, too!

(To leave a review go to the product page on Amazon, scroll down and select
"Write a customer review")

Let's be friends! - CONNECT *and* SHARE *with us*

We would be thrilled to hear (read) about your journal ideas, or other comments &
suggestions you may have. And if you would like to be part of our "launch team",
to receive free samples of future journal concepts, please let us know, too!

Instagram: @adaytoremember_journals
Amazon: follow "A Day to Remember Journals"
or email us at: adaytoremember.journals@gmail.com.

And please "tag us" on Instagram when you post about your experiences!
WE WOULD ♡ TO BE PART OF OUR JOURNEY
the same way we feel that you are a BIG part of ours!

xoxo, Carla and Milena

How to use this Journal

** Important Facts and Events of your Life **

Use this space to make notes about the most important facts and events of your life. You will be guided by the questions on the pages.

Your Special Recommendations for your Grandkids

On this section, in addition to recommendations, you will have space to add your thoughts and share feelings about things that happened in your life and in the world during your lifetime.

These are thoughts and feelings that may or may not relate to the memories told on the previous pages, but that are part of your way of living and thinking. For instance, you may want to...
- share your thoughts about some of the world leaders at your time,
- encourage your grandchildren to stay engaged in causes that matter to you (eg. climate change, diversity and inclusion),
- or you may want to share some baking tips,
- advice for them to be financially savvy,
and more.

** Selected Memories & Stories Pages **

Remember how many stories happened in your life that you would like to share with your grandchildren? This is the space for that.

On these pages you can choose the memory / story you want to tell, describe it in detail and even (if you'd like) paste any image, photo, or piece of something that you kept from it. It will be a beautiful journey!

Use your creativity and share a piece of who you are with your grandchild....

Let's get started...

Important Facts & Events of your life

The Story of:

Add your name or nickname here

When and where were you born? How was your birth?

Who are/were your parents & grandparents? Write a little bit about them...

Where did your family come from? From which country or region? Are there any interesting facts about your family history?

What was happening in your country and in the world when you were born, growing up and as an adult?

Where did you spend your childhood? What were your favorite places?

What were your favorite games and books as a child?

Let's write a little bit about the schools you went to, and how were your experiences there.

Who were your best friends when you were a kid or a teenager?

Did you go to college? If so, where and when? How was that experience?

Did you work outside the house? If so, talk about the places where you worked. What are your feelings about your professional choices?

How did you meet grandpa?

Did you get married? If so, how was it? How was life together?

How many kids did you have? When were they born and how was it for you and grandpa to expand the family?

What are your kid(s) names? Share an interesting fact about their lives. (If my mom or dad is the only one, share some interesting things about his/her life!)

How was your life when you were a mom? What were your favorite things - and least favorite ones - about being a mom?

How did you find out that you were going to become a grandma? How did you feel then?

How is your life now that you are a grandma? What are your plans for your life and for you and me/us (your grandkid or grandchildren) to do together?

Your Special Recommendations for your Grandkids

If you could recommend your grandchildren a book and a movie, what they would be and why?

If you could recommend a place to visit, where would it be and why?

If you could recommend your grandchild a hobby or something that you love to do, what would it be and why?

If you could recommend a recipe or cook something with your grandchild, what would it be?

When did you eat this? In what situations? With whom?

If you could share your views on world leaders and your political beliefs, what would they be?

What are the causes that you are / were engaged in or passionate about? Why are they important for you & your grandchildren? (eg. Climate change, Diversity)

If you could give some financial advice what would it be?

If you could teach or say something to your grandchildren, what would it be? Try to write a letter on important things that you want him/her/them to know.

Selected Memories & Stories

Date:

Share a story in which you had to face a big obstacle, but with persistence, you were able to overcome it. What lessons did you learn?

Space for a picture or any "piece" of the memory that you may have saved (eg. Newspaper article, sticker, an old handwritten note...) or some additional notes about the world when it happened.

Date:

Share a story in which you were pleasantly surprised.

Space for a picture or any "piece" of the memory that you may have saved (eg. Newspaper article, sticker, an old handwritten note...) or some additional notes about the world when it happened.

Date:

Share what are the things that makes you the happiest. Tell me about a very happy day.

Space for a picture or any "piece" of the memory that you may have saved (eg. Newspaper article, sticker, an old handwritten note...) or some additional notes about the world when it happened.

Date:

What is something you wish you had done (or had already done) in life that you'd recommend me to do (sooner)?

Space for a picture or any "piece" of that recommendation that you may have saved (eg. Newspaper article, sticker, an old handwritten note...) or some additional notes about the world when it happened.

Date:

Share stories of the moments in your life when you learned something important. (It can be as a kid, as a teenager and as an adult.)

Space for a picture or any "piece" of the memory that you may have saved (eg. Newspaper article, sticker, an old handwritten note...) or some additional notes about the world when it happened.

Your Choice of Selected Memories & Stories

In the final part of this section,
we invite you to freely choose
the stories that you'd like to share...

Let your grandkids know about the
most special or
remarkable moments in your life and
these special moments that you shared with him/her, too
- those that should be carried through generations...

Date:

Memory/Story that you'd like to share today:

Describe a little bit this memory/story.
Why is that memory important to you? How do you feel about it?

Space for a picture or any "piece" of the memory that you may have saved (eg. Newspaper article, sticker, an old handwritten note...) or some additional notes about the world when it happened.

Date:

Memory/Story that you'd like to share today:

Describe a little bit this memory/story.
Why is that memory important to you? How do you feel about it?

Space for a picture or any "piece" of the memory that you may have saved (eg. Newspaper article, sticker, an old handwritten note...) or some additional notes about the world when it happened.

Date:

Memory/Story that you'd like to share today:

Describe a little bit this memory/story.
Why is that memory important to you? How do you feel about it?

Space for a picture or any "piece" of the memory that you may have saved (eg. Newspaper article, sticker, an old handwritten note...) or some additional notes about the world when it happened.

Date:

Memory/Story that you'd like to share today:

_____

Describe a little bit this memory/story.
Why is that memory important to you? How do you feel about it?

Space for a picture or any "piece" of the memory that you may have saved (eg. Newspaper article, sticker, an old handwritten note...) or some additional notes about the world when it happened.

Date:

Memory/Story that you'd like to share today:

Describe a little bit this memory/story.
Why is that memory important to you? How do you feel about it?

Space for a picture or any "piece" of the memory that you may have saved (eg. Newspaper article, sticker, an old handwritten note...) or some additional notes about the world when it happened.

Date:

Memory/Story that you'd like to share today:

Describe a little bit this memory/story.
Why is that memory important to you? How do you feel about it?

Space for a picture or any "piece" of the memory that you may have saved (eg. Newspaper article, sticker, an old handwritten note...) or some additional notes about the world when it happened.

Date:

Memory/Story that you'd like to share today:

Describe a little bit this memory/story.
Why is that memory important to you? How do you feel about it?

Space for a picture or any "piece" of the memory that you may have saved (eg. Newspaper article, sticker, an old handwritten note...) or some additional notes about the world when it happened.

Date:

Memory/Story that you'd like to share today:

_____

Describe a little bit this memory/story.
Why is that memory important to you? How do you feel about it?

Space for a picture or any "piece" of the memory that you may have saved (eg. Newspaper article, sticker, an old handwritten note...) or some additional notes about the world when it happened.

Date:

Memory/Story that you'd like to share today:

Describe a little bit this memory/story.
Why is that memory important to you? How do you feel about it?

Space for a picture or any "piece" of the memory that you may have saved (eg. Newspaper article, sticker, an old handwritten note...) or some additional notes about the world when it happened.

Date:

Memory/Story that you'd like to share today:

_____

Describe a little bit this memory/story.
Why is that memory important to you? How do you feel about it?

Space for a picture or any "piece" of the memory that you may have saved (eg. Newspaper article, sticker, an old handwritten note...) or some additional notes about the world when it happened.

Date:

Memory/Story that you'd like to share today:

Describe a little bit this memory/story.
Why is that memory important to you? How do you feel about it?

Space for a picture or any "piece" of the memory that you may have saved (eg. Newspaper article, sticker, an old handwritten note...) or some additional notes about the world when it happened.

Date:

Memory/Story that you'd like to share today:

_____

Describe a little bit this memory/story.
Why is that memory important to you? How do you feel about it?

Space for a picture or any "piece" of the memory that you may have saved (eg. Newspaper article, sticker, an old handwritten note...) or some additional notes about the world when it happened.

Date:

Memory/Story that you'd like to share today:

Describe a little bit this memory/story.
Why is that memory important to you? How do you feel about it?

Space for a picture or any "piece" of the memory that you may have saved (eg. Newspaper article, sticker, an old handwritten note...) or some additional notes about the world when it happened.

Date:

Memory/Story that you'd like to share today:

Describe a little bit this memory/story.
Why is that memory important to you? How do you feel about it?

Space for a picture or any "piece" of the memory that you may have saved (eg. Newspaper article, sticker, an old handwritten note...) or some additional notes about the world when it happened.

Date:

Memory/Story that you'd like to share today:

Describe a little bit this memory/story.
Why is that memory important to you? How do you feel about it?

Space for a picture or any "piece" of the memory that you may have saved (eg. Newspaper article, sticker, an old handwritten note...) or some additional notes about the world when it happened.

Date:

Memory/Story that you'd like to share today:

Describe a little bit this memory/story.
Why is that memory important to you? How do you feel about it?

Space for a picture or any "piece" of the memory that you may have saved (eg. Newspaper article, sticker, an old handwritten note...) or some additional notes about the world when it happened.

Date:

Memory/Story that you'd like to share today:

Describe a little bit this memory/story.
Why is that memory important to you? How do you feel about it?

Space for a picture or any "piece" of the memory that you may have saved (eg. Newspaper article, sticker, an old handwritten note...) or some additional notes about the world when it happened.

Date:

Memory/Story that you'd like to share today:

_____

Describe a little bit this memory/story.
Why is that memory important to you? How do you feel about it?

Space for a picture or any "piece" of the memory that you may have saved (eg. Newspaper article, sticker, an old handwritten note...) or some additional notes about the world when it happened.

Date:

Memory/Story that you'd like to share today:

Describe a little bit this memory/story.
Why is that memory important to you? How do you feel about it?

Space for a picture or any "piece" of the memory that you may have saved (eg. Newspaper article, sticker, an old handwritten note...) or some additional notes about the world when it happened.

Thank you For Using This Journal. We Hope you liked it!

We are on a journey of publishing 52 journals this year!
We would love to invite you to check out one of our other Journals:

E English **F** French **G** German **I** Italian

Therapy Journals

THERAPY JOURNAL:
E F G I

This is a journal with prompts (questions and suggestions), and it was designed to support you during 30 therapy sessions, no matter how often they take place (ie. it will be ok if you use it twice a week, once a week, or once every 2 weeks). It also includes important recommendations that will help you make the most of your therapy sessions.

ONLINE THERAPY JOURNAL:
E F G I

Similar to the above, this is a journal with prompts (questions and suggestions), and it was designed to support you during 30 virtual / telephonic therapy sessions, no matter how often they take place (eg. twice a week, once a week, or once every 2 weeks).
The difference it that this journal gives recommendations for VIRTUAL sessions.

THERAPY SESSIONS JOURNAL:
E F G I

If you like to write in LINED journals, this is the one for you! This journal also has prompts (questions & suggestions), and it was designed to support you during 6 months of therapy (with weekly therapy sessions, ie. 4-5 sessions per month). This therapy journal will help you make the most of your therapy and self-reflection sessions.!

COUPLES THERAPY JOURNAL:
E F I

This journal has 3 main spaces for you to write in: (1) a space for you to write what is the focus of each session , (2) a space to capture how your partner is thinking and feeling and what he/she is sharing, (3) and finally a space for you to write your own insights & takeaways during counseling sessions. The right choice for people attending Couples Therapy!

Therapist Journal

A THERAPIST JOURNAL:
E F I

Encouraged and guided by a professional therapist, we created this journal to provide the best help for therapists, both in their preparation for the therapy sessions, and during the sessions themselves.
This journal is what we were told would be the most efficient way for organizing therapist notes, all in one place!

Inner Peace, Resilience & Relationships

HAPPINESS FROM THE SOUL
F I

This "self-therapy" happiness journal is exactly what you need to start to implement daily 3 things that a Harvard professor teaches : Organize your errands / Message someone important/ Write a journal entry. After a few days doing this, you're very likely to start feeling happier!

GRATITUDE, AFFIRMATION AND MANIFESTATION JOURNAL
E F G I

This journal brings it all to you: Gratitude, Affirmation & Manifestation. They together can emanates the best feelings within us and help us become calmer, more resilient and in turn help us live a happier life and give us the encouragement to pursue our goals.
This journal will help you relax and connect with the best within you to create the life of your dreams .

Kids

LET'S GO READING JOURNAL FOR CHILDREN:
E F I

This journal was created to encourage kids to have reading & discussion time with their grown ups. It also includes key recommendations for the grown ups on how to make the most of reading time with kids. And the "big readers" will have a wonderful record of the child's assisted reading journey.

SUMMER READING JOURNAL FOR CHILDREN:
E F

This child-friendly journal will help caregivers and children establish a reading routine during this summer. After going through the challenge of 25 books this summer, kids will learn to look forward to reading & discussion time, and the "big readers" will have a record of the child's reading progress made over time! This journal also includes a list of suggested activities for the summer

KIDS ACTIVITIES JOURNAL FOR CHILDREN:
E

This journal was designed to support families in developing a healthier, more organized & efficient routine of activities while raising their children. It will help you plan for playful activities, games & hobbies with children, in addition to encouraging them to do school work and help with chores.

Motherhood, Fatherhood & Family

MOMMY & ME A KEEPSAKE JOURNAL
(E)

This is a journal with prompts that will guide a mother to write about her memories and prepare her children to thrive in life by learning mom's important advice & lessons.
Fill any page, at any time, until you complete the journal, or feel that "it's ready". Then give it (back) as a treasured gift to your child!

GODMOTHER, YOUR STORY IS A GIFT JOURNAL
(E)

A godmother's gift & godchild's gift!
This journal with prompts will guide a godmother to write about her treasured memories and important recommendations that she would like to share with her godchild.
Fill any page, at any time, until you feel that "it's ready" to be gifted to your godchildren.

GRANDMA, YOUR STORY IS A GIFT JOURNAL
(E)

The best gift for grandma!
This journal will prompt a grandmother to write about her memories, special moments with the grandkid, and precious advice. Grandmas will love to share their story, and when "ready" this journal will be a treasured gift to future generations!

AUNTIE LOVES YOU FOREVER JOURNAL
(E)

This is a journal with prompts that will guide an auntie to write about her memories and prepare her nephews & nieces to thrive in life by learning important advice and lessons. Fill any page, at any time, until you complete the journal, or feel that "it's ready". Then give this precious gift (back) to your nephews & nieces!

THINGS I LOVE (AND NOT SO MUCH) ABOUT BEING A MOM:
(E) (F) (I)

This is a blank / lined journal for moms to write about motherhood experiences – good and bad days – and make the most out of all of their days. It will help you normalize what's normal, feel more relaxed and clear your mind. And over time you will have a beautiful collection of "motherhood moments"!

FATHER YOUR STORY IS A GIFT JOURNAL
(E)

This is a journal with prompts that will guide a father to write about his memories and prepare his children to thrive in life by learning dad's important advice & lessons.
Fill any page, at any time, until you complete the journal, or feel that "it's ready". Then give it (back) as a treasured gift to your child!

PRIDE FATHER, YOUR STORY IS A GIFT JOURNAL
(E)

This is a journal with prompts that will guide a father to write about his memories and prepare his children to thrive in life by learning dad's important advice & lessons.
Fill any page, at any time, until you complete the journal, or feel that "it's ready". Then give it (back) as a treasured gift to your child!

GRANDFATHER JOURNAL. A GRANDPARENT MEMORY BOOK
(E)

The best gift for grandpa!
This journal will prompt a grandfather to write about her memories, special moments with the grandkid, and precious advice. Grandpas will love to share their story, and when "ready" this journal will be a treasured gift to future generations!

... and more!

Check our full collection on Amazon.

⭐ ⭐ ⭐ ⭐ ⭐

Journals available in other Languages

Our journals are available on Amazon in English, German, French and Italian
(with more languages to come soon).

Join our "Launch Team"

**If you would like to to receive free samples of future journals to help us
validating concepts, with cover visual selection and more, please let us know!**

--> *New journals are launched almost every week!* <--

Connect with us & leave your Review on Amazon

**If for any reason you are not satisfied with your journal,
please contact us directly;
we will do our best to make you happy!**

*And, especially if you're happy with the journal,
we'd really appreciate if you could leave an honest review on Amazon
(even just the star rating helps us a lot!)*

**We would love to stay connected, and receive your comments or suggestions.
Follow / message / tag us / leave a review:
- on Amazon: A Day to Remember Journals
- Instagram: @adaytoremember_journals
- OR email: adaytoremember.journals@gmail.com.**

*With much gratitude,
Carla and Milena*

Made in the USA
Monee, IL
16 November 2021